Patina Style

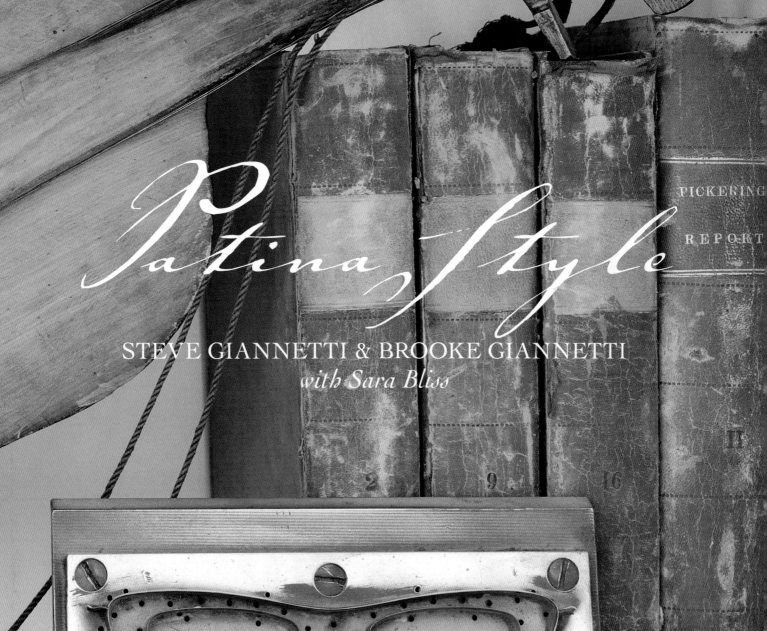

Patina Style

STEVE GIANNETTI & BROOKE GIANNETTI

with Sara Bliss

PICKERING

REPORT

To our three beautiful children, Charlie, Nick and Leila.

Our dearest thanks are to our children, for it is through the life we share with them that our Patina Style philosophy emerged.

Thank you to our parents for their constant support and encouragement; to our friends, design colleagues and fellow shop owners for enriching our lives and inspiring our work.

Thanks to our amazing clients, who share our vision of what is beautiful and trust us to design their homes, and our fantastic Giannetti Home design team, who help us turn our dreams into reality every day.

We're grateful for all of the talented people who played a part in creating this book: Jill Cohen, our dear friend and book agent, who believed in Patina Style from the minute she first stepped into our shop; the amazing Doug Turshen and his team for creating a gorgeous layout from our thousands of images; the incredibly talented writer Sara Bliss, who turned our casual morning chats into eloquent prose; writer Laurel Kornhiser, who expresses the essence of Patina Style in the introduction of this book; photographer Lisa Romerein, who captures our work so beautifully in her images; Kate Burger for her fabulous styling; and our Gibbs Smith editor, Madge Baird, who seamlessly brought all of the parts together to create the book that was previously only in our dreams.

A special thank-you to all of our Velvet and Linen readers, who have joined us on this journey and whose support and understanding made this book a reality.

INTRODUCTION

Life isn't about the things you own but about the experiences you have with them. Patina Style embraces the *life* in things: the newel post worn smooth where hands always land, the leather trunk that bears the rubs and scratches of global travel, velvet that is faded, silver that is tarnished, or a flowerpot embedded with moss. This is the essence of Patina Style, a design philosophy that has evolved through our own lives, both personal and professional.

It all began when, after years of designing for other people, we had the opportunity to relocate our offices, redecorate our home, and open a store. Rather than one of us taking the lead, we visited antique shows and swap meets together and bought the items that we both loved. We designed furniture we wanted but couldn't find anywhere. We brought all the elements that we had collected together,

and a new look emerged, featuring aged fabrics, gilded objects, rich leathers, roughened woods, and industrial artifacts. Our personal style began to come forth as a reflection of our personalities. That special chemistry that is created from the dynamic interplay of opposites, masculine/feminine, simple/ decorative, industrial/gilded, came together; as in a marriage.

Patina Style also grew from a desire to add meaning and calm to our surroundings. It was born of a palette of warm neutral colors—soft creams, gray-greens, and calm blues—that create serenity. We gravitated towards materials that felt real and that age gracefully over time—pine or oak floors, plaster walls, and natural finishes. We chose objects that showed the artist's touch and the creative process at work. We wrote about the transformations on our Velvet and Linen blog. As we wrote, our design philosophy was clarified. Positive comments followed, magazine inquiries came and we developed the ideas further.

We have asked ourselves why our style resonates with so many; why people respond to the beauty of Velvet and Linen; why the flea market items and antiques that we feature in our store, Giannetti Home, strike such a reverberating chord. When we bring antiques and other artifacts from the past into our homes, we connect with the stories behind them, the people who created and used them. That's what people love about countries like Italy and France—the idea that these places have a patina, or history.

Objects also carry the history of people's interactions with them and the effects of nature on their surface. We have three wonderful children and know that the typical decorated home is not compatible with a real family's life. In fact, the imperfections that come from or kids dinging the floors and the furniture come to mean something different to us. Just like the patina of a fine antique can be celebrated, our own family patina becomes important. We come to cherish the wears and tears of life, to know things are precious precisely because of their imperfections.

We challenge the conventional wisdom that it's easier to play it safe. We want to create spaces with emotional impact, spaces that celebrate the beauty in the old, the imperfect, the slightly roughed- up. We are not antique experts. In fact, we prefer not to know an item's provenance but to react to it

These Swedish antiques capture our love of rustic and refined, and their beautiful gray color is one of the foundations of our palette.

viscerally. On our frequent excursions to flea markets and antique stores, we buy things because we love them, because they have great proportions, beautiful styling, simplicity, and a sense of history.

We design with the whole family in mind. Children need places that both serve a purpose and ignite curiosity. A children's study can spring from the idea of creating a workshop for learning, starting with a steel gray wall to enclose the space and old wooden library chairs, framed vintage photos of Europe, and industrial lighting to transport them to a simpler past, while the laptop poised on a newly minted metal desk keeps things current. Yes, a family room or children's study needs to be indestructible, but it can still be sophisticated, surprising and engaging.

Our design philosophy extends outdoors as well. Architectural elements like shutters, columns, fountains, and corbels define outdoor spaces. We design gardens like the rooms in our home—with furniture, lighting and wonderful antiques. The outdoors finds its way into our homes as well, blurring the line. Outdoor shutters or a garden element placed inside creates a casual, warm feeling.

Throughout the book, you will come to understand why we believe personal expression and style are so important. We will show how we do things like repurpose salvaged objects, bring outdoor furniture indoors, turn something old into something better than new. We hope it will inspire you to do things your own way, to follow your heart, to seek beauty in your life. When you follow your own unique perspective, you will love the results.

Like a patina itself, our design style has evolved and deepened over time. Still, our primary goal to create an emotional response has not changed. Velvet and Linen has given us a chance to directly connect with people who have commented on our efforts and viewed our work online. Our blog has touched people in ways we couldn't have imagined when we started it. We've had people tell us that it has helped them cope with sickness and adversity, that the beauty and personal expressions are inspiring and meaningful to them. Out of design has come a deep connection to each other, to our clients and to our online friends. In *Patina Style*, we are excited to continue sharing the beauty we see in pieces with a past and the magic of creating spaces that enhance the way we really live.

The pink inside this vintage drop-down desk is a lovely surprise and a wonderful example of why we always prefer the unique quality of antiques to reproductions.

Embracing Imperfection

We are drawn to pieces that show their age—the rustic elegance of a worn finish or the alluring appeal of an artfully faded fabric. We see past, present, and future in vintage objects and old houses. Older pieces with character and history are far more exciting and interesting to us than anything new or mass-produced.

We love wandering through flea market stalls and navigating the tight aisles of antique stores, searching for whatever catches our eye. We are drawn to furniture and architectural elements that show the effects of time: wood weathered to silver-gray, bleached to blonde, or darkened to imperfection; mahogany brown and camel-toned leathers; distressed plasters; faded fabrics; and tarnished metals. We connect with these timeworn objects emotionally, and we associate this connection with their colors.

Although these antiques hail from different parts of the globe, they are unified by a common palette.

Beautifully weathered pieces

celebrate the passage of time.

Palette

To create the Patina Palette, we start with subtle colors that elicit a purely emotional response and then we layer in real, honest, and vintage materials that become even more exquisite with time. Intriguing and weathered colors, finishes and materials work together to create a mix of rustic and refined. We draw our palette from the landscape, as well as objects we love, to create a soothing refuge from the frenetic world. The thoughtful combination of understated natural hues and textures in our palette provides a beautiful backdrop for your life.

We like to ground larger pieces in natural fabrics and neutral colors.

Inspired by Nature

When we are developing a color scheme, we look to the outside and bring those hues indoors. For our coastal California home, our many long drives up the coast inspired us to surround ourselves with a beachy palette. Plaster walls and cream-colored linen sofas are echoes of soft white sandy beaches. Timeworn faded carpets with hints of oceanic blues add soothing touches of color. The varied gray tones of driftwood are seen in weathered wood tables, bark-colored seagrass, vintage baskets, aged wood floors, and stone-colored linen upholstery.

This mellow backdrop lets all the pieces breathe a bit, allowing your eye to move to the accents—just like in nature. Darker neutral touches, like worn camel-colored leather, tobacco-toned woods, and steel gray accessories, provide contrast and add some masculine energy to a room. Watery aquas pull in the blues and greens of the sea as it fades towards the horizon. Celadon and chalky grays from the garden continue to blur the line between indoors and out. The magic is that we respond to natural colors indoors the same way we do when we are at the beach or in the garden—they create a relaxed and happy atmosphere.

The juxtaposition of distinctive textures and shapes—glossy shells,
matte coral and aged glass bottles—create a work of art.

Paint

Our goal is to create an instant emotional response to the spaces we design, and color has the incredible ability to do that. We are particularly drawn to the power of quiet colors—muted taupes, soft grays, ethereal whites. The calm hues that we surround our clients with provide an immediate sense of peace—a wonderful contrast to their hectic lives.

In our bathroom, the burlap curtains and the pale pink walls echo the palette of the flea market flamingo painting and its aged wood border.

When we select paint for rooms, we look for luminescence, transparency, and muted tones. We have a special preference for Farrow and Ball paints because of the incredible way their natural pigments interact with light. Walls painted in natural pigments seem to change color as the light shifts during the day. For example, under bright sun, a beige color might resemble the shade of beach sand, but under shadow it becomes a darker taupe. We prefer calm, chalky colors rather than vibrant tones. If a color comes on too strongly right out of the can, we simply sand it to softness. We will often dilute paint and apply it with a rag to achieve a more transparent finish. This technique can be used to great effect over unfinished wood to achieve instant aging. Color, finish, and technique can all be used to add depth and dimension to paint, giving you endless possibilities.

We strive to create the feeling of being surrounded by color, so we prefer to paint walls, trim and ceiling in the same tone. More often than not, people simply paint their ceilings white by default. But unless the walls are white, a white ceiling has no connection to the walls below, making it look like an afterthought. Painting the whole room the same color creates a cocoon effect. Another option is to visually play with the dimensions and feeling of a room by mixing fifty percent white into the wall color and painting that new lighter shade onto the ceiling. This softer shade makes ceilings appear higher—a great solution for a room without a lot of architectural height.

In this bedroom, we painted one wall with a single accent color and then sanded it to achieve a chalkier aged patina.

In our children's study,
a collection of vintage
world tour photos takes
center stage due to the
calming effect of painting
the walls, trim and
ceiling the same color.

LIGHT

Light is an important factor to consider when choosing a color, as it can completely transform the look of a hue. A color that livens up a room in one space can be dull and depressing in another—all due to the amount of light a space receives. What direction a room is facing, how big and how many windows, the height of the room, the view—all of those factors affect the light, which affects color. Think of light as adding an extra tinge of color to whatever shade of paint you choose. For example, in a west-facing room, a color will appear a bit more yellow, while a north-facing space will invite a touch of blue. In a sundrenched room, darker shades can make a room feel warmer and richer, while on the flip side, in a dark room, a soft, light-catching paint can be like a spotlight that lightens up and expands the space. Looking at a color in both daylight and nighttime is essential to selecting the right shade.

Steve's paintings capture the magical, ever changing
pairing of the light and water just outside.

Texture

From the perfect simplicity of burlap to the more elegant softness of silk, we are drawn to textures that become more beautiful with age and are wonderful to touch. We love pairing everyday fabrics like linen with more sophisticated ones such as velvet, as they play off each other perfectly. Vintage fabrics, especially ones that look as if they have been touched thousands of times, are a wonderful addition to a room. We celebrate the places where velvet is crushed and where cottons are worn; texture tells a story.

Unlike man-made fibers that have chemicals and stiffness, we prefer natural fibers that are washable, soft and family friendly. We often use stonewashed or Belgian linen slipcovers on chairs and sofas. For the beds, we prefer the droopy and inviting look of white or cream linen. Because of its warm earthy color, burlap is a casually chic option that works as well for upholstering an ottoman as it does for curtains. Another textile staple of ours is painters' drop cloths from Home Depot (yes, really!). Prewashing softens the cloths so they feel like old homespun linen, but at a fraction of the cost. The velvets we use are either vintage and a little tattered, or newly loomed, imperfectly, on handlooms in Europe. For silks, we adore hand-stenciled versions from Fortuny that bring an old-world elegance to a room.

Pillows and bed linens are like artwork on a bed: they add extra detail and color.

Floors

We gravitate toward wood floors that get better with time. To get the look of an old factory floor in our shop, we chose quartersawn white oak, which shows less grain than traditional oak floors. We finished it with one coat of water-based sealer. The floor gets better looking each year as the finish wears off and time leaves its mark.

For our Santa Monica house, we wanted to install wide-plank pine floors that looked like those in 1920s beach cottages. We chose a mix of eight-foot-long pine shelving boards in a variety of widths then glued and nailed them down directly to the plywood subfloor. To give the pine floor the distressed, aged look we wanted, we lightly rolled the edges with a metal pipe.

We often rely on these nubby jute carpets for their soft, natural texture
and the wonderful backdrop they provide for layering carpets.

For finishing wood floors, we prefer water-based sealers or natural wax-based versions, as polyurethane yellows over time and has a fake shiny quality. Natural bees wax, on the other hand, gives floors a subtle luster. Unless you have a brand-new floor with too much polyurethane, we don't recommend refinishing; we prefer floors that look distressed. Use wood throughout the house, even in bathrooms and kitchens; wood always brings warmth and softness to a space.

STONE AND TILE

Most people tend to over-design a stone or tile floor because there are so many choices for patterns, mosaics and liners. We avoid all of this complexity and focus on choosing stunning natural materials that don't need a lot of embellishment. One of the most cost-effective surfaces is travertine tile. While it is sold in twelve-by-twelve-inch squares, we cut these in half, using smaller pieces for walls and the larger ones for the floor. Travertine comes in great colors from pale beige to walnut brown and looks best when installed in a simple pattern.

Limestone is another favorite of ours. At Oxnard we have large slabs of French limestone on the shower walls. Aged limestone has a distressed surface that is just perfection. In a Malibu project, we covered the outdoor patios and swimming pool surround in French limestone and then carried it throughout the house. One of our staple materials is Carrara marble. It makes the classic bathroom floors in a hex mosaic. We also love Carrara for counters in kitchens and embrace the imperfection that enhances Carrara counters over the years.

You cannot go wrong with timeless, three-inch-by-six-inch white subway tile, either flat or beveled. While subway tile is sold at a low price, caps, corner edges and bullnoses are at a higher cost; so go with a simple cap, base, and quarter rail top if you want to save more money. Another good tile option is glass. We've especially liked baths done in three colors of blue glass tile mixed together to re-create the effect of light reflecting on the water.

Wide-plank pine boards nailed to the subfloor are a gorgeous flooring option that only gets better with time.

RUGS

Seagrass, sisal, and jute are hallmarks of the understated elegant look we love. They add beautiful natural texture and the prices are within reach. In projects where installing a wood floor would be too costly, we often go with a tightly woven wall-to-wall seagrass. Seagrass is one of the least expensive rugs you can find, and it almost acts like wood, developing a beautiful weathered gray-brown patina over time.

Sisal brings a lot of light into a room. The yellowish tone of sisal tricks your eye into believing that there is sunlight in the space. Sisal is also easy to find at various price points, from Pottery Barn to Ikea.

We've also discovered the beauty of chunky jute rugs. Softer than sisal, jute is a wonderful alternative in bedrooms and spaces where you spend a lot of time in bare feet. If you're afraid of stains, a pet stain remover called Get Serious is a natural-fiber-carpet lover's best friend.

Some people would throw out a rug that has been bleached by the sun, but we adore the faded look of worn vintage carpets. Rugs with intense, deep shades draw too much attention to the floor and ultimately look heavy. We prefer carpets with a neutral background and chalky beiges, blues, and greens. We often place the rugs upside down, as the colors on the underside are often more muted (see page 40). Tabriz and Oushak carpets from the Middle East have airy graphic patterns in neutral shades that are good complements to the Patina palette.

We like rugs that have the same quality as aged velvet. They might have once been vibrant, but now the hues have mellowed.

Walls

We like walls to have character, to glow ever so slightly, and feature the wonderfully imperfect patina of walls you would find in an older house. To get this look, we spread a plaster topping finish called California One Kote over drywall. This process yields breathtaking results! Walls have a more permanent, aged look and become luminous without looking too shiny or glossy. One Kote's cool white tone has more depth than paint, and provides a crisp, multifaceted backdrop.

We explain to our contractors that making a wall perfectly smooth takes the life out of it, like refinishing an antique to make it look new. Quite the opposite, we embrace the rawness that occurs in the early stages of a project. We like to see evidence of the work involved and the trowel strokes, and we don't polish or sand that away. To give our Santa Monica house the character of an old beach cottage, we used an undulating application of One Kote over the drywall and barely sanded it.

WALLPAPER

From grasscloth to scenic florals, wallpaper helps set the tone of the room and provides a beautiful backdrop. We often use grasscloth on walls because we love how it surrounds a room with warmth and texture. Grasscloth also has a wonderful ability to capture and reflect light. One of our favorite papers is a Whitewashed Madagascar, as it has the natural color of jute and perfectly complements our palette. There are hundreds of shades of grasscloth, including ones with a bit of shimmer that is perfect in a dining room to create walls that sparkle under candlelight.

We also love de Gournay hand-painted wallpapers. While they are a bit expensive, the dreamy landscape and floral scenes give rooms an illusion of depth—like looking at an expansive vista through the walls. The versions painted on silk have a glow, while the rice paper backgrounds feature a cool, chalky finish.

The natural color of the grasscloth wall paper complements our favorite collections.

Elements

One of our favorite ways to create original spaces is to incorporate vintage architectural elements in our rooms. Often large in scale, architectural items like corbels, beams, and fireplace mantels have a big impact on the feeling of a room. From the antique pine door that greets guests when they arrive, to a dining room wall lined with weathered outdoor shutters, these elements are a powerful way to inject some unique personality into a home. Whether you hang a vintage clock face as art or choose to build elegant bookshelves in your bedroom, the details you add become beautiful visual expressions of your style. At the end of the day, that is what you want your home to be—an expression of you.

If you live in a house where there is little to no architectural interest, introducing salvaged architectural details brings both warmth and a lovely richness. In our Santa Monica home that we built eight years ago, the oversized corbels mounted under the ceiling and the vintage fireplace mantels look as if they are part of the structure of the house. We want all of our spaces to have that feeling of history you find more often in older homes.

At our beach house, antique Swedish doors were redesigned to create a closet and a place to display Steve's drawings.

Large-Scale Elements

When you are designing a room, you have to begin with the large elements. Start with pieces that can give a room some presence, such as a big carpet, or vintage doors hung on the wall. If you start with the little things, you will get caught in a magnifying glass focus that will prevent you from seeing the big picture. Whether it is a large clock or an oversized piece of art, a couple of large elements are important to ground a room.

We salvaged an old church window, put mirrors in place of the glass, and a fabulous focal point was born.

We love to discover the
stories behind the vintage
pieces we buy, like the fact
that this clock face was once
the clock in the town square
of a small village in France.

SALVAGED DOORS

We look for doors that have a beautiful patina. We prefer aged pine—faded to a gorgeous sandy hue—not the yellow of new pine. We also love weathered gray antique oak doors.

There are two ways we like to incorporate salvaged doors. One way is to replace standard interior or exterior doors with them to add a bit of history to a house—always a good trick for getting out of the cookie cutter new-house rut. Another option is to simply hang them against a blank wall and celebrate the beauty of the doors. In our Oxnard dining room, we placed two old pine doors on a wall, like art, and then we hung paintings on top. It feels like a beautifully paneled section of the room and brings a delightful depth to the space (see page 54).

Doors with an aged patina make a rich backdrop for furniture and collected objects.

These salvaged doors add interest to a blank white wall when hung as art and layered with 1920s flea market paintings.

Antique pine doors from France create the perfect backdrop.

BOOKCASES

Unembellished floor-to-ceiling bookcases, lined with worn leather books, are a nice way to bring some charm and architectural character to a space. We like to place them on either side of a window, with a cozy window seat in between creating the perfect nook for curling up with a good book.

A less pricey alternative to custom bookshelves is to use one-inch-by-twelve-inch boards between two pieces of wall. We love the simplicity of these types of shelves, shown on page 61.

Another idea is to craft a bookcase out of something else entirely, like we did in our bedroom at Oxnard. There we transformed an antique arched Swedish door and shutters into a bookcase/closet. We reconfigured the piece, turning the shutters into the main doors and adding slim bookshelves inside. We built two boxes on either side and added shelves and mirrored doors. Having this wonderful large element in the room really balances the space, plus we love the additional storage and the beautiful aged patina of this piece, seen on page 47.

To tie a large element like a bookshelf to the whole room, we often paint or wallpaper the back of the shelves. We frequently choose chalky colors as our backdrop—green, gray, blue—or we line the back of the shelves with grasscloth wallpaper for rich, neutral texture.

A monochromatic palette transforms the individual objects in a pair of bookshelves into one powerful and united visual element.

SHUTTERS

Maybe it is the graphic punch that comes from the layering of wood, the worn patina from years spent facing the elements, or the complexity and texture that they bring into a room, but vintage shutters are magical. It's unexpected to see outside material used indoors, and that magnifies the effect these shutters have on a room. We have discovered so many interesting and distinctive ways to use them indoors.

While shutters add a charming architectural element to a space, we also rely on them to help mask a room's flaws. In our Oxnard house, for example, we placed four large shutters along a wall in the breakfast room to cleverly provide the illusion of windows where there are none. Using shutters to cover actual windows is a wonderful solution for a window that is poorly proportioned or has a terrible view. This allows a bit of light to come in and creates a new and better focal point. Shutters can also be used to widen the look of a window when one (or several) are placed on either side—a good design trick to use if a window is too small for a wall.

We love the layering effect of hanging paintings or plants, on top of the shutters, as it makes them part of the architecture of a room rather than just a focal point.

FIREPLACES

Nothing exudes style, warmth, and charm quite like a fireplace mantel. However, most of the new mantels are too large or too heavy and have a tendency to overpower a space. We've found the way to avoid that bulky look is to either make our own mantels or source antique Italian and French versions. We gravitate towards ones made from limestone, as they tend to be less formal and have the clean elegance we like. If the firebox isn't exactly the same shape, we surround the firebox to the edge of the mantel with black slate, which makes the firebox appear larger.

For wood mantels that we design, we are inspired by the simplicity of classical door surrounds. The simplest of our mantels are merely a piece of casing surrounding the mantel with a crown molding on the top (example on page 5). Another version we often use has flat columns of wood on either side, with nice crown molding at the top. We treat mantels like any other large-scale element in a room, often distressing the painted finish or using an aged material such as used brick (see overleaf).

Vintage shutters have so many fun and interesting uses indoors.

Three-hundred-year-old Flemish panels hung on bookcases add a refined touch to a casual beach house living room.

64

Windows

Windows connect you to the outside, tying the interior to the exterior. If a window is placed incorrectly, too high for example, you are disconnected from the outside. It's wonderful to be able to see the outside from any point in the room instead of a cropped view. We prefer low windowsills: twelve inches from the ground is really ideal, with the top almost at the ceiling. Windows on two sides of a room perfectly balance the light.

Window treatments can go a long way towards fixing any flaws that might be part of the room. We mount matchstick blinds a foot above the top of a window to give the illusion that the window goes higher than it does (see page 68). Placing shutters or draperies on either side also visually enhances the width of the space, making it seem as if the windows are wider than they are.

We lean towards natural cottons and linens for window treatments because they diffuse the light that comes through the window. In the public rooms, we never use blackout shades because translucent gauzy treatments make the light much nicer. We prefer slim 5/8-inch iron rods because we don't want the rods or the curtains to be the focal point of the room. Instead we want your eye drawn to the outside.

FRENCH DOORS

One of the best ways to bring light into a room is to replace standard interior-exterior doors with glass French doors. It is a great trick to maximize light, one you'll especially appreciate if you live in a house with minimal natural light. At our house in Santa Monica, we installed French doors throughout the interior, and the space is brighter and filled with wonderful coastal light as a result. This is especially noticeable in our hallways, where there is an abundance of natural light even when doors are closed (see page 70). For interior doors, we favor milk glass panes, which provide privacy but also allow sunlight to flow from room to room.

A trick when you have French doors that are too short is to hang matchstick blinds right above them to make the door appear taller.

Trim and Molding

Our house in Oxnard was built in the 1970s, and one of the first things we removed was the clunky trim that was popular during that decade. Removing the trim visually calmed down the whole house. If your trim has the wrong proportions, we recommend removing it. Painting the trim and molding the same color as the walls can help in allowing these elements to fade into the background.

We found these porch columns with fading house numbers at a flea market when we were building our house. We like how they add an interesting architectural detail to the room.

Lighting

"Light the walls not the floor" is our motto. To achieve a beautifully illuminated space, we avoid recessed lighting. Instead, we prefer the ambient light provided by chandeliers, wall sconces, and table and floor lamps. Light-colored shades create a softer glow than darker versions, so we always choose shades in cream and white.

Half shades work incredibly well on sconces because they shoot light back onto the wall, as in our bedroom at Oxnard. For chandeliers, we choose versions that aren't too ornate but have character, like the shell chandelier in our dining room. In another project, two oversized basket shades above a long dining table worked perfectly. Lining the fixtures with a soft gauze added some femininity to their masculine shape (see page 85).

In kitchens we often use industrial holophane pendant lights. Made of ridged glass and metal, these fixtures provide the perfect filtered light needed over a center island.

Because our Oxnard kitchen has a very low ceiling, we placed table lights on the island counter and drilled a hole under each one for the cord.
Facing: Industrial holophane pendant lights give a vintage kitchen a modern uplift.

Antiques & Furniture

As much as we appreciate the allure of vintage objects, we believe that truly delightful rooms strike the right balance of old and new. We design for real lives and real families, and new pieces add comfort, solid construction, and durability—important qualities for bustling households.

However, for a sense of history and uniqueness, you can't beat antique furnishings. We recommend featuring at least one old piece per room. Vintage pieces add layers of visual interest to a space—they absolutely make a room sing.

The new pieces we use are often upholstered ones: beckoning sofas, comfortable armchairs, and understated headboards. There needs to be places where the eye can rest, and neutral upholstered pieces provide that beautifully. Covered in light colors, these become background pieces, letting the antiques and artwork stand out and shine.

The combination of the feminine lines of Brooke's grandmother's silver leaf chairs paired with our masculine leather Frasier chairs brings a fresh energy to the dining room.

Welcoming Entries

Entries should be more than just places that people quickly walk through. They need to offer convenient storage and places to put down keys, bags, mail—all the essentials you carry into the house. In our entry, we built a wall of lockers so everyone has his or her own designated place for things. Inside each locker we have hooks for the kids' backpacks and shelves for storage.

Entries also need a staging place, and tables or even low walls provide a perfect perch. Remember to include entry seating, someplace to put on shoes, pull off a pair of boots, or wait for the family to get ready. The addition of seating and tables make an entry feel like a room in itself, rather than simply a place to pass through.

When buying antiques for our stores or clients, we only choose pieces we would want to have in our own home, like this ornate antique Swedish bench.

We think of living and family rooms as spaces where family members can be together, even when they are involved in different pursuits. We design these spaces to allow for multiple activities. Someone can lounge on the sofa while someone else is on the computer and another family member might be having a late dinner and watching TV. We often place a desk behind a couch to serve as a place to eat, work, and surf the Web.

We try to breathe life into living rooms, turning them into more than just rooms for sitting. Too often, formal living rooms are reserved for formal occasions that rarely happen. Instead of creating a room that is usually empty, we often design the living area with additional uses. Objects including musical instruments, game tables, and extra bookshelves filled with a variety of books take some of the formality out of the space and opens it for multiple purposes.

When choosing sofas, we like them long enough to recline on but not overly bulky. Finding versions to fit the bill is challenging, so we began designing our own. We create sofas that are understated and elegant, up to nine inches shallower than some of the newer types. Our sofas are filled with down-wrapped foam to retain their shape and provide maximum comfort. Slipcovering sofas makes for easy cleaning, and the slipcovers we design fit snugly against the sofa for a more sophisticated look.

Chaises, armchairs, and benches provide additional places to lounge. We love putting benches right in front of the fireplace. We also like the versatility of ottomans that can work as seating as well as a perch for feet or as a table.

Occasional tables can add a lot of character to a room. Consider vintage trunks and baskets as interesting options for tables, maybe a little stone piece or a garden table. Stacks of books can also work as an unexpected side table.

*A table for eating or playing games shares space with chairs placed
for conversation, allowing multiple uses in a family space.*

This eighteenth-century
Swedish cabinet was the
first piece that we fell in love
with for the living room, and
it became the inspiration for
the rest of the space.

Lively Dining Rooms

Our ideal dining room is one that promotes a comfortable atmosphere, where people like to gather. This space is as likely to be the setting for a lively dinner party as it is a place to work on a school project.

The shape of a room dictates the style of dining table, but we often source round ones, as they are more conductive to great discussions. Another option is a long farmhouse table—a bit more casual and especially functional for large gatherings for children and their friends.

Twenty-nine inches is an ideal height for all dining tables, as it promotes a casual and comfortable dining experience. Shorten your tables and you will see a difference! We like to mix all types of seating at the table—benches for long tables, slipcovered chairs for easy cleanup, and masculine-style leather chairs. The key is to avoid the overscaled bulkiness that so many of the new chairs carry. Instead, look for slimmer pieces or vintage chairs that have a narrower silhouette.

Combining distinctive finishes and materials always adds fresh energy to a space. A dining room, where the focus is on a few major elements, is an ideal place to experiment with different pairings. We avoid matching dining sets and instead focus on a dynamic interplay of unexpected combinations: a vintage stone pedestal topped with glass; a rich, dark wood table contrasted with slipcovered chairs in a light fabric; a group of wood chairs partnered with a zinc-topped table. In one project, we combined industrial, Swedish, and garden elements to create an informal yet elegant dining room.

Clean-lined furniture gives the dining area character, and an unexpected pairing of gauzy linen with an oversized industrial metal frame makes the light fixture a favorite of ours.

Soothing Bedrooms

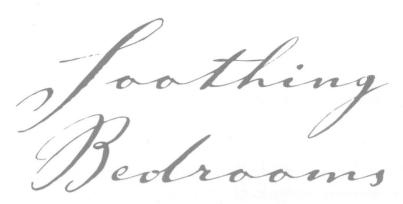

Bedrooms should be emotionally quiet spaces. To achieve this serenity, we rely on a monochromatic palette that includes an inspired mix of comfort and texture. Choosing neutral and soothing colors ensures a visually calm environment.

Because you touch everything in this space, it should be filled with only very soft and tactile fabrics. We adore the quiet colors of cream and white bedding in an assortment of textures such as matelasse, cotton and linen. For our bedroom, we have fallen in love with Matteo Tat bedding, made

A vintage Italian ornament was a gift from Steve for the holidays. Paired with a simple linen headboard and understated bedding, it is a romantic focal point for the bedroom.

of gorgeous linen with slightly torn ruffled edges because it features that perfect pairing of rustic and refined. In lieu of a bed skirt, we placed a king Tat duvet cover under the mattress. We keep bedding simple and add interest with pillows made of wonderful vintage textiles or a special hand-loomed velvet—they are like little jewels on a bed.

A traditional headboard is not the main focus of our bedrooms. We prefer a simple white linen headboard, putting the emphasis elsewhere. In both of our bedrooms, we have placed beautiful visual details above the bed. In our Oxnard bedroom, we placed a stunning Italian wood scroll above the linen headboard to add some interest in a room that had no architectural details. In Santa Monica, we hung a corona lined with antique Fortuny fabric, and it has become a romantic, old-world focal point in the space (see overleaf).

To keep things interesting, we avoid matching side tables, as they feel too contrived. We use tables that are the same height and provide a drawer or two for storage. Baskets filled with snuggly blankets are often placed underneath our bedside tables.

When designing a room we like to create cozy areas that allow us to live in a way that we dream about. For instance, we had a dream of having quiet dinners in front of the fire in our bedroom, so we placed a little table and chairs there. Now it has become a little romantic getaway in our own house. If you have a couple of kids, sometimes your bedroom is the only place you can call your own, even if only for a few minutes.

Adding a chaise, a sofa, or a really comfy chair in your bedroom will provide a relaxing space— for flipping through magazines, taking a little nap, or just daydreaming.

Plants and flowers can instantly add a touch of romance, subtle color, and life to a space.

We ignite curiosity with varieties of textures and pieces from the past.

Warm Bathrooms

We treat bathrooms like every other room in the house, embellishing them with art, antiques, rugs, furniture, and warm textures. If you ignore all the expected notions of what a bathroom should be and think about designing your bathroom the way you would any space that you want to enjoy, you'll love the results. Try a vintage cabinet and baskets for storage instead of built-ins. Hang a pretty mirror in lieu of a basic medicine cabinet and surround it with art. Think of the tub as a piece of furniture—look for a beautiful tub with great lines. You can even repurpose a vintage cabinet as a sink, as we did with a Swedish version, for a one-of-a-kind piece (page 94).

We avoid the coldness often associated with porcelain and tile used in bathrooms by choosing alternative materials. We love the warmth that comes from wood floors and have not experienced the warping that people fear. We also adore the feeling of a pretty antique rug against bare feet. Curtains in burlap, linen and cotton also add wonderful texture.

Don't forget to include a place to sit—for dressing and undressing, having a conversation, or just enjoying a moment of peace. If you have ample room, try a cozy loveseat; if you have less space, an ottoman goes a long way.

And, finally, paint the bathroom a color that is both flattering and calming, something other than stark white. We painted our Santa Monica bathroom seashell pink and love the results (page 96).

This stunning hand-polished pewter tub is both functional and gorgeous.

We really wanted to create the dreamiest bathroom we could imagine—the pink walls, tufted ottoman, and burlap curtains all combine to create this instantly soothing space that we both adore.

Inspired Offices

People often believe that having a small desk in the kitchen is ideal. But the reality is, a kitchen desk is usually too narrow and faces a wall. It becomes a target for clutter, and a busy kitchen is a tough place to get anything done. Instead, try locating your office somewhere beautiful, where you have room for everything and where you can focus.

When we moved Brooke's office from a desk in the kitchen into the sunroom, it made use of a previously neglected room. This fantastic sunlit area features a view of the garden and plenty of storage space. It's ideal for busy days blogging and designing! Brooke switched to a deeper thirty-inch-deep desk, which provides ample space for a laptop and papers. She is cocooned at her desk in the cozy Clive wing chair that Steve designed. The desk is placed in the middle of the room to take advantage of the natural light and to enjoy the view. Two baskets on the floor hide a printer and paper. A large cabinet behind the desk provides closed storage as well as clear glass cupboards for showcasing interesting accessories, books, and magazines.

In our children's study, vintage industrial tables provide an indestructible working area. Stacked baskets and vintage wood boxes allow easy access to necessities like tape, markers, and scissors. The vintage library chair was purchased at a local swap meet. Trunks, artists' boxes, toolboxes, and vintage lunch pails are unexpected yet practical options for storing supplies (see page 28).

Note that in both of our home offices, most of the items weren't originally intended for an office—we didn't purchase furniture from an office or container store. Instead, we found furniture and accessories that we loved and repurposed them for a space that is both aesthetically pleasing and also functional.

This is Brooke's space to design and dream. Her desk used to be in the kitchen but she traded it for the sunroom—the best room in the house.

*Brooke uses the vintage desk
with a feminine silhouette
as a place to write notes or
get ready for a night out.*

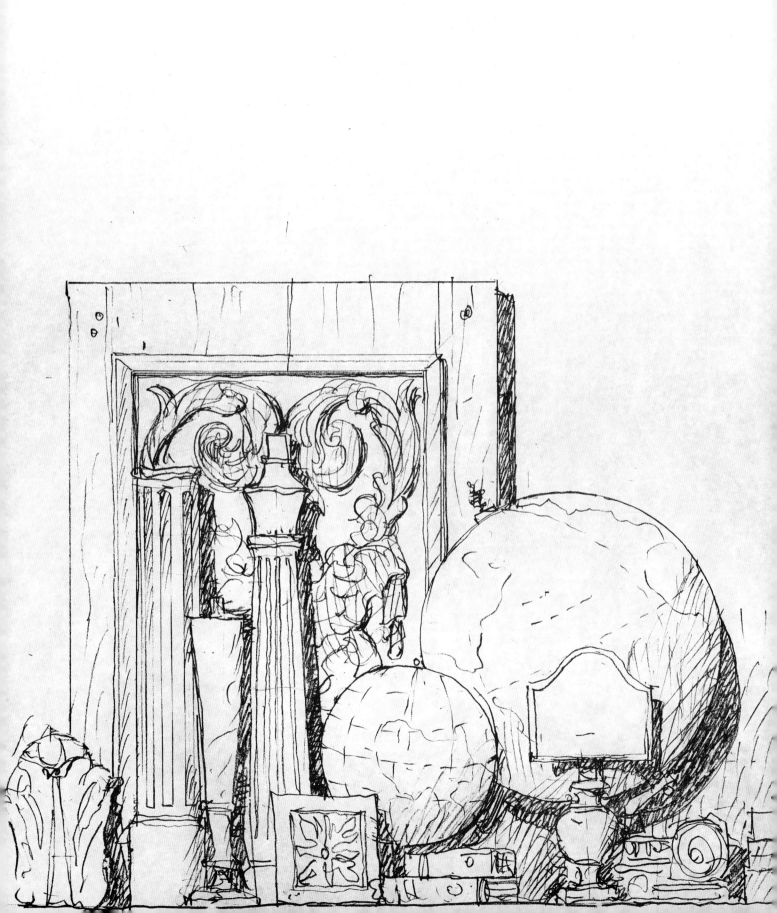

Collect and Display

There is such a thrill that comes from finding things you want to display in your home. The most appealing collections are those that have been gathered over time. There is something slightly forced about buying a dozen new things in an outing and then displaying them. It is much more intriguing and organic to assemble objects d'art, curios and accessories that have special meaning to you. The woven textile you found on your trip to Morocco, or the vintage clown college trophies you discovered at the flea market.

Collections should start with the one piece that really intrigues you: an antique board game, a stunning landscape, a gorgeous piece of hotel silver—anything you find so alluring that you want to have more. Then, over time, you keep your eye out for additional pieces—at flea markets, antiques stores, swap meets, on eBay, or on your travels—buying only the ones that really resonate with you. The result will be a collection that has weight, meaning, and memories.

Three dissimilar collections work comfortably together in this unique arrangement.

Navigating Flea Markets

At flea markets; you just never know what you are going to discover. Interesting portraits, antique spools, vintage textiles—there is an endless array of treasures to find. However, because there are so many stalls and so many objects, flea markets can sometimes be overwhelming. To navigate the visual clutter, it helps to go with specific items in mind, even written on a piece of paper tucked into your pocket. Then you will be able to hone in on what you are looking for rather than becoming distracted.

On the flip side, it's also fun to sometimes browse flea markets without any expectations at all, letting the different aesthetics and philosophies of each vendor inspire you. We think the vendors are truly design trendsetters, often collecting objects that they feel a strong connection to and curating them in an unexpected way. There's something intoxicating about being around people who are passionate about the pieces they sell and who bring their individual design perspectives to their stalls. We enjoy seeing the beauty of things through their eyes, as it gives us new ideas for how to display objects, how to combine them and how to live with them.

The beauty of flea markets is that they are filled with unexpected surprises.

French shop boxes. 35 cm.

Massing Volume

In order for you to really have a collection, you need volume. One clock face is a pretty object, but if you have several, there is much more of an impact. Grouped together, individual pieces become like one big object, making a striking visual statement. With most objects, only when you have gathered about four or five of them does it start to feel like a collection. Smaller objects, like vintage pocket watches, need to be grouped in even bigger numbers to really attract attention.

*Objects and paintings with a similar theme have more
impact when displayed in a group.*

Organizing the Display

When grouping different objects or paintings, they must have a strong link to really work as a whole. The most common mistake people make is just placing things randomly on shelves, which results in a cluttered look. We've found that putting like-minded things together—by color, type, or theme—calms a room visually.

Try not to limit what you think a piece can be. This desk is a terrific storage piece for a dining room. The drawers hold sugar packets and tea bags, while the shelves display white china.

Combining collections to form an artful vignette is our favorite way to display.

114

LIKE OBJECTS

One foolproof way to create a display is to showcase similar objects together. However, they can be similar in a variety of ways, and that is where your artistic eye comes into play. The likeness might be in color, or shape, or period style, or material, or place of origin. At home, we have ten vintage globes lined up on a special shelf above our TV. They are mostly from the 1940s and are all in the same neutral tones. To keep the arrangement interesting, though, we chose globes of varying sizes, and we love the look that resulted from this grouping (see overleaf).

A collection of similar items can be displayed in many creative ways.

COLOR

Mixing pieces in the same hue creates one big display. At Oxnard in Steve's office, shelves feature baskets, cogs, and worn leather books, all in warm brown tones, for a graphic effect. You don't have to choose pieces in precisely the same color to make this work; just the same general shade results in a subtle layered complexity.

Linking by color is also a great trick with paintings. If you hang paintings having a similar color tone, they will emanate a particular mood. We've found that paintings from the same time period, like the 1940s paintings we are so often drawn to, work perfectly together because they have similar palettes (see overleaf).

ARRANGING BY THEME

Displaying objects or paintings by theme is a fun approach. In our Oxnard living room, Steve's *Water Series* paintings on the wall are linked not only by their blue and green palettes, but also by their soothing subject matter. When hung together, with the same amount of space between them, the water paintings become a larger, very expressive statement.

We've also had success with grouping objects by themes in larger bookcases. For one client's game room, we placed vintage toys and carnival games on different shelves, linked by their playful spirit. We've done the same with vintage instruments for a family that loves music. But we did limit the color palette with both of these: for the games we went with vibrant hues toned down by the neutral books in the shelves, while the musical instruments tended to be in calmer hues (shown on page 116). When done right, themed collections can add a lot of character to a space.

The turquoise shades in Steve's Water Series *paintings inspired the colors of the decorative accessories.*

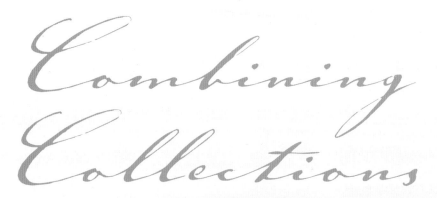

Combining Collections

Three is a magic number when it comes to displaying distinct objects together. Three things are not so many that your eye gets overwhelmed, and they are just enough to form an intriguing composition. For example, we layer Steve's travel watercolor sketches on shelves with pretty pieces of decorative plaster, punctuated by the shiny vintage pocket watches. As always, we keep things in the same color range. And since we are often drawn to soft, muted and neutral hues, this makes it easy to mix and match, keeping the focus on shape and texture. We frequently have leather or parchment books in our arrangements because they are very neutral, blending beautifully with a lot of different pieces. They also provide good perches for layering and height.

When creating a display on shelves, we always place the large elements first and then fill in with smaller accents.

Creating a Composition

There are a few compositional rules that can help you when you are putting things together. Think of it as balancing a scale. The visual weight of one side of your arrangement should match the visual weight of the other. One way to achieve balance is by symmetry—making the two sides mirror reflections of each other. Another way is to start with the larger grounding elements of a composition, like books, and then counterbalance the weight on the other side with pieces that, while different, match the books in visual interest. Then you can fill in the display, making sure there are objects at different levels and sizes to keep the eye flowing. You place a tall element and then a larger, wider element and keep layering until it works. We make a point to not have things be too perfect. Your arrangement is ready when you step back, look at it as a whole, and love the way it looks.

When creating displays, the truth is that you have to feel more than think. The best advice we can give is to take all the rules of what works, process them, and then go with your instinct. Sometimes you just need to stop the chatter in your head that holds you back from your creativity. Experiment. Move things around. Try things in a different way. In the end, you'll know when you get it right; you will feel it.

Several collections and a few large-scale vintage objects
are composed in an intriguing vignette.

Indoor
Outdoor

We approach outdoor spaces with the same attention to detail that we give to designing interiors. We think of these spaces as outdoor rooms and design them to be as beautiful, useful, and individual as their interior counterparts.

We rely on tall trees, hedges, gates, shutters, trellises, and antique doors to act almost like walls, defining where the spaces begin and end. Then we develop the structure of the room, adding plants, placing interesting objects as focal points and, finally, artfully arranging furniture and accessories. The result is an al fresco space that reflects the same sense of relaxed elegance as the homes we design.

We really wanted to connect this powder room to the pretty garden just outside, so we incorporated a stone floor, a marble sink, and an old garden spout into the space.

Our front yard initially looked like anyone else's with a little piece of grass in the front. Now it's our vegetable garden, where we grow organic vegetables and fruits. We thought, Why not?

Formal Informal

Balancing formal organization with the informality of nature is the key to designing magical outdoor spaces. The formal structures go in place first: gravel walkways, defined flower beds, low stone walls, stone floors, and boxwood hedges are all beautiful ways to add structure and definition to a garden. One of our favorite ideas is to use broken concrete slabs to create low walls and paving, a decidedly less expensive alternative to stone (see page 151).

Once you've established structure, focus on letting the space go a little wild. Scatter plants and flowers in pretty weathered pots throughout. Give certain planting areas a bit of an informal feel with looser plants—lavender, rosemary, and floribunda roses are lovely picks. Choosing the best plants to lend an informal, organic feeling to the room depends to some degree on what climate zone you're in and what plants thrive there, as well as your color preferences.

The French doors on our garage echo the look of a guesthouse
and allow it to double as a party pavilion.

Patina Plants

When designing our gardens, we select plants and flowers in muted shades of soft purples, faded pinks, pale gray-greens, and wonderful whites. We limit the palette to just two or three different colors, along with abundant green. This philosophy is consistent with the color palette we use indoors. We prefer the harmony that comes from soft shades, without the visual noise of too many competing colors.

There are a few plant and flower varieties that we turn to again and again to create the patina garden. A large profusion of white and pale pink hydrangeas infuses the garden with color. White floribunda roses bloom in a very dramatic way. Wisteria, with its cascade of purple blooms in spring, is also magnificent. Jasmine or lamb's ear are terrific ground cover options. To create a visually interesting garden, we select plants in a range of heights.

We love using succulents in pots because they are low-maintenance and introduce a variety of bright green shades. We are especially fond of aeoniums, with their daisy-shaped greenery. Lavender, sage and rosemary are plants we rely on for color and amazing aroma. Miniature boxwood hedges provide a verdant, formal backdrop in a garden.

For mid-level heights, we adore potted citrus and kumquat trees as well as ornamental apple and pear trees. Jasmine and rose vines have a fantastic fragrance and look incredible growing on houses, trellises and fences. Cecil Bruner is a favorite rose vine, displaying a profusion of miniature pink flowers. In Santa Monica, our front palm trees serve as trellises for white floribunda rose vines.

For larger elements, sycamores, California peppers and oak trees are solid choices in our area. We often use birch trees because of their beautiful gray-and-white bark; these look especially nice along a pathway.

We have English cabbage roses, angel's trumpet, and two varieties of aeoniums in our garden.

Floors for the Outdoors

One way to define and separate distinct outdoor areas is to change the ground cover. Grass acts like a soft outdoor carpet that unifies the overall space. Stone and gravel walkways become like hallways, leading you from one place to the next. A stone stairway provides a transition space with character. For a rustic walkway or for a romantic pool surround, we love the rough edges of broken concrete surrounded by an inch or two of grass.

We recycled the concrete we tore up from our old driveway,
using the pieces to create garden paths.

Furnishing Outdoor Rooms

It all starts with a vision of how you want to live in your outdoor spaces. Do you want to have big family dinners? Lounge by the fire? Take in the view? Paint? Write? Entertain? Read? Play Games? Once you've analyzed your lifestyle and needs, the next step is to activate the space with furnishings and accessories that will allow you to turn your dreams into reality.

For our Santa Monica kitchen garden, we created an area for Brooke to pot plants, arrange flowers and cut herbs. Recognizing how much she loves these gardening activities, we knew that we needed a bench to sit on, outdoor shelves for storing pots and supplies, and big tables for prepping and arranging.

Furnishing your rooms with purpose in mind gives the spaces heart and soul. In our Oxnard garden, we wanted to provide a cozy place to lounge by the fountain, along with a place to savor a cup of tea or enjoy a nice breakfast together. So we placed wicker chairs with big pillows by the fountain, along with two little cafe chairs and a stone table. Now we use that space all the time (page 148).

Mixing materials is essential to designing an intriguing space, and certain materials hold up beautifully under the elements (though not all will withstand the harshness of freezing winters and snow). We like the texture of wicker, especially the warm gray of real wicker aged over time. Strong woods like teak, faded to that weathered gray, are especially appealing. Lightweight iron, metal, and stone tables all bring different patinas to an outdoor room.

When selecting fabrics, we like to incorporate lovely textures and pale hues through pillows and upholstery. Options for outdoor fabrics have gotten softer over the years, and there is a wide range of patterns to choose from. Outdoor linen is one of our favorites, and it comes in an array of warm shades, neutrals and earth colors being our favorites.

This patio room is designed as a true blending of indoor and outdoor uses.

Garden Accents

We like the surprise of incorporating decorative elements that you wouldn't normally expect to find outside, such as paintings. We hang paintings on porch walls, layered on vintage doors or shutters—but always underneath an overhang to protect them from the rain. Artwork really completes an outdoor living space, making it feel like a harmonious extension of the interior.

Garden elements like vintage gates, planters, sculpture, wheelbarrows, and weathered pots can enhance the overall style. Vintage birdcages have a whimsical look that appeals to us, and we arrange plants, paintings or other architectural elements inside them, creating little vignettes.

Whether you choose romantic pieces like old stone sculptures, or architectural ones such as stone columns with mercury orbs, accessories add wonderful dimension to the garden.

A vintage birdhouse provides a wonderful garden home for potted plants.

Weathered French shutters add warmth to our garden.

148

Fire and Water

There is something spectacular about sitting outdoors next to a roaring fire. Its warmth allows you to enjoy the outdoors long into the night. Plus, everybody looks great in the romantic glow of a fire.

There are two types of fireplaces we like to incorporate into al fresco rooms. On a porch or under cover, a fireplace with a mantel is an elegant focal point that blurs the lines between indoors and outdoors. We also love a gas-lit fire pit. It replicates the feel of a campfire and its perimeter walls offer an ideal perch for sitting or for serving. If you center a gas fire pit between sofas or other seating, you can put a wood cover over it and use it as a coffee table during the day.

The combination of fire and water is a powerful one. We've designed spaces with a fire pit below and a fountain above, surrounded by stacked concrete. The combination can act as a focal point during both the day and the evening.

The power of fire is contained within a wall of broken concrete slabs,
while water is contained by an antique cement fountain.

Outside In

One method of linking outside and inside is to use outdoor furniture like stone, teak, and iron pieces inside the house. A teak dining table, wicker stools, metal chairs and stone side tables introduce a relaxed garden atmosphere to your rooms. In our powder room at Oxnard, we chose a fountain spout in lieu of a faucet and a marble planter is used instead of an ordinary sink. Topiaries enliven the space, and a glass panel door connects the room to the garden outside. The space feels like a continuation of the garden with these unexpected outdoor pieces (shown on page 135).

We like to include something living in the rooms we create. To encourage a connection to nature, we often incorporate topiaries in moss-covered, aged pots. We add taller plants, such as rose, olive or ficus trees for a larger scale element in the room. In our bedroom, a potted rose tree adds a beautiful canopy to the seating area. A bouquet of cut flowers from the garden placed on a side table or a large massing of newly dried hydrangeas above the mantel brings more of the garden inside (shown on page 67).

Beakers from a science lab, picked up at a swap meet, make pretty vases to hold roses from the garden.

$\mathcal{W}$e started this journey by bringing together all the things that we loved and paying attention to all the items that had real meaning in our life. We wanted to see where it took us. It was a leap of faith. Neither of us has any formal interior design training, so we were free to combine elements in ways that intuitively felt right to us. A style is personal, and in this book we have tried to explain where ours came to life and why it has meaning to us. We hope we have inspired you in some small way to see your home in a different light and create your own personal Patina Style.

RESOURCES

Giannetti Home
11980 San Vicente Blvd
Los Angeles, CA 90049
www.GiannettiHome.com
www.Patina-Style.com

FLEA MARKETS AND ANTIQUES SHOWS

Alameda Point Antiques and Collectibles Faire
Alameda, CA
www.antiquesbybay.com

First Sunday of every month. Wear your most comfortable shoes. This market is huge!

High Point Market
High Point, NC
1.800.874.6492
www.highpointmarket.org

Although High Point is known mainly for it's new furniture lines, many fantastic antiques dealers participate as well. Check out Tara Shaw and others at the Suites at Market Square.

Long Beach Outdoor Antique and Collectibles Market
Long Beach Veterans Stadium
4901 East Conant St
Long Beach, CA 90808
www.longbeachantiquemarket.com

Third Sunday of every month.

Pasadena Community College Flea Market
1570 East Colorado Blvd
Pasadena, CA 91106
www.pasadena.edu/fleamarket

First Sunday of every month.

Pasadena Rose Bowl Flea Market
Rose Bowl Stadium
Pasadena, CA
www.rgcshows.com/RoseBowl for
Rose Bowl general information

Second Sunday of every month.

Santa Monica Airport Flea Market
Santa Monica Airport
off Bundy Drive

Fourth Sunday of every month. It's small but good.

Scott Antique Market
Atlanta Expo Center
3650 Jonesboro Rd SE
Atlanta, GA 30354
www.scottantiquemarket.com

Collectibles. Visit our favorite vendor, Jill Dineen, for fantastic European treasures, including vellum books and gorgeous creamware.

ANTIQUE COLLECTIVES

A Beautiful Mess
28875 West Agoura Rd
Agoura Hills, CA 91301
818.874.9092
www.abeautifulmessantiques.com

As their website states, A Beautiful Mess is "where antiques, design and oddities meet pure and simple elegance."

Agora Antique Mart
28863 Agoura Rd
Agoura Hills, CA 91301
818.706.8366
www.agoraantiquemart.com

Although this is a smaller antiques collective, the vendors always provide inspiration with their quickly changing vignettes.

Foxglove Antiques and Galleries
699 Miami Circle
Atlanta, GA 30324
404.233.0222
www.Foxgloveantiques.com

The Foxglove antiques dealers fill this collective with gorgeous antiques from around the world. Because they get new shipments every week, there is always something new to see.

Summerland Antique Collective
2194 Ortega Hill Rd
Summerland, CA 93067
805.565.3189
www.summerlandantiquecollective.com

Whenever we travel up the California coast, we always pop in to this large collective. They often have some great architectural pieces. We've also found several of our best vintage ship paintings here.

Wertz Brothers
1607 Lincoln Blvd
Santa Monica, CA 90404
310.452.1800
www.wertzbrothers.com

Twenty thousand square feet filled with over 100 different vendors. The merchandise turns around quickly, so there is always something new to see! Many inspiring displays.

ANTIQUES AND ARCHITECTURAL ELEMENTS

Atelier de Campagne
3010 Center St
Soquel, CA 95073
www.atelierdecampagne.com

We first discovered Atelier de Campagne at the Alameda Flea Market. Owners Trinidad Castro and Johan de Meulenaere import unique items from Europe, including beautifully worn shutters, garden elements, and antique furniture.

Big Daddy's Antiques
13100 South Broadway
Los Angeles, CA 90061
310.769.6600

1550 17th St
San Francisco, CA 94107
415.621.6800
www.bdantiques.com

One of our favorite resources for industrial furniture and architectural elements. Owner Shane Brown travels around the world and fills his warehouses with unique one-of-a-kind pieces.

Charme d'Antan
29963 Mulholland Highway
Agoura Hills, CA 91301
818.889.0229
www.charmedantan.net

Charme d'Antan is a fantastic resource for limestone fountains and mantels, as well as gorgeous antique French doors and architectural pieces.

Eloquence
1618 Stanford St, Unit A
Santa Monica, CA 90404
310.453.5503
www.eloquenceinc.com

Owners Amelia Cooke and Kim Redmond fill their warehouse with French antiques and their French-inspired furniture line. To the trade only.

Giannetti's Studios
3806 38th St
Brentwood, MD 20722
301-927-0033

Beautiful plaster ornament and molding.

Lief
646 North Almont Drive
Los Angeles, CA 90069
310.492.0033
www.liefalmont.com

Swedish brothers Stefan and Michael Aarestrup have created something special. Each piece they select is a piece of art, whether it be Swedish baroque or ancient Chinese.

Linda Horsley Antiques
425 Peachtree Hills Ave, Suite 11A
Atlanta, GA 30305
404.467.0001
www.horsleyantiques.com

We can't imagine visiting Atlanta without stopping by Linda's store.

Love Train
3640 Jonesboro Rd
Atlanta, GA 30354
404.271.8630
www.lovetrainantiques.com

Located just below Scott Antique Market, Love Train was an unexpected surprise. Owner Mark Sage loves mixing beautiful Swedish antiques with rustic industrial finds. To the trade only.

Rue de Lillie
2496 Lillie Ave
Summerland, CA 93067
805.695.8180

Walking into Rue de Lillie is like being transported to France. Don't miss the gravel courtyard behind the cottage, where several vintage birdcages are home to a flock of cooing doves.

Tone on Tone
7920 Woodmont
Bethesda, MD 20814
240.497.0800
www.tone-on-tone.com

A great resource for stunning Swedish antiques.

TEXTILES

Benison Fabrics
8264 Melrose Ave
Los Angeles, CA 90046
www.bennisonfabrics.com

Wonderful authentic English hand-printed fabrics.

Claremont Furnishing Fabrics
1059 3rd Ave, 2nd Floor
New York City, NY 10021
212.486.1252
Fax 212.486.1253
www.claremontfurnishing.com

Made on European vintage looms, their fabrics have a wonderful imperfection and authenticity that usually can be found only in antique textiles. I use their Velours Silk Velvets as accent pillows on beds and sofas to add elegant depth and texture. To the trade.

Cowtan and Tout
8687 Melrose Ave, Ste B-647
Los Angeles, CA 90069
310.659.1423
www.cowtan.com

Lovely classic English fabrics.

D. Bryant Archie
www.dbryantarchie.com

Our favorite alpaca pillows and throws.

Libeco Linen
www.libeco.com

True Belgian linen in fantastic weathered, muted colors.

Thomas Lavin
8687 Melrose Ave, Ste B-310
Los Angeles, CA 90069
310.278.2456
www.thomaslavin.com

C&C Milano, available at Thomas Lavin.
www.cec-milano.com

World Linen and Textile Co.
1350 East Washington Blvd
Los Angeles, CA 90021
www.worldlinen.com

A great resource for inexpensive basic linen.

BEDDING

Matteo
912 East Third St
Los Angeles, CA 90013
213.617.2813
www.matteohome.com

Our favorite is their tattered yet elegant "Tat" linen. To the trade only.

FINISHES

California One Kote
www.westernblended.com

An inexpensive alternative to plaster.

Farrow and Ball
8475 Melrose Ave
West Hollywood, CA 90069
323.655.4499
www.farrow-ball.com

We love their chalky color palette and the way their full spectrum paints react with the light in a room throughout the day.

PLUMBING FIXTURES

Waterworks
Viktoria Urbanas
8580 Melrose Ave
West Hollywood, CA 90069
vurbanas@waterworks.com
www.waterworks.com

The most gorgeous plumbing fixtures. They are truly jewelry for the bathroom.

STONE AND WOOD FLOORS

Contempo Floor Coverings
902 South Barrington Ave
Los Angeles, CA 90049
www.contempofloorcoverings.com

Our favorite resource for gorgeous wood floors and seagrass carpets.

Exquisite Surfaces
289 North Robertson Blvd
Beverly Hills, CA 90211
www.xsurfaces.com

Fantastic selection of new and antique limestone and wood floors. Their antique and reproduction mantels are stunning!

First Edition
15 14 13 12 11 5 4 3 2

Published by
Gibbs Smith
P.O. Box 667
Layton, Utah 84041

1.800.835.4993 orders
www.gibbs-smith.com

Designed by Doug Turshen with David Huang
Printed and bound in China

Gibbs Smith books are printed on paper produced from sustainable
PEFC-certified forest/controlled wood source. Learn more at www.pefc.org.
Printed and bound in China

Library of Congress Cataloging-in-Publication Data

Giannetti, Steve.
  Patina style / Steve Giannetti & Brooke Giannetti with Sara Bliss. — 1st ed.
    p. cm.
  ISBN 978-1-4236-2253-6
  1. Giannetti, Steve. 2. Giannetti, Brooke. 3. Interior decoration—United States—
History—21st century. I. Giannetti, Brooke. II. Bliss, Sara. III. Title.
  NK2004.3.G53A4 2011
  747—dc22
                                                                  2011009117